Hand Lettering God's Word for Girls

JENNY HIGHSMITH

HARVEST Kids
HARVEST HOUSE PUBLISHERS
EUGENE, OREGON

To my children—
May your hearts forever be filled with the truth of God's Word and the joy of creativity. This book is a testament to the love and inspiration you bring into my life each day. May these pages be a source of light, learning, and laughter as you grow, explore, and color your world with wonder.
With all my love,

Mom

Cover and interior design by Nicole Dougherty

For bulk, special sales, or ministry purchases, please call 1-800-547-8979.
Email: CustomerService@hhpbooks.com

This logo is a federally registered trademark of the Hawkins Children's LLC. Harvest House Publishers, Inc., is the exclusive licensee of this trademark.

Hand Lettering God's Word for Girls
Copyright text and artwork © 2025 by Jenny Highsmith
Published by Harvest House Publishers
Eugene, Oregon 97408
www.harvesthousepublishers.com

ISBN 978-0-7369-8970-1 (pbk)

Printed in the United States of America

25 26 27 28 29 30 31 32 33 / VP / 10 9 8 7 6 5 4 3 2 1

Contents

INTRODUCTION

A Note to Young Artists

Hey, budding artists and creative minds! Ever wondered about the magic of hand lettering? It's not just about writing some words down on a page. Hand lettering is about turning your words into art, making them dance and sing with your unique style. So let's jump into the colorful world of hand lettering and discover how it's more than just a skill. It's a supercool way to bring your imagination to life!

Hand lettering is just a fancy kind of cursive. So why should you learn fancy cursive? Let me tell you a few reasons.

1. Magical Letters That Spark Your Creativity:
Imagine your words turning into magic on paper! Hand lettering is like using a wand to create beautiful letters that are uniquely yours. Each swirl and curve is like a spell that makes your writing come alive. It's not just about writing; it's about turning your words into a magical masterpiece!

2. Crafty Fingers, Stylish Moves:
Learning hand lettering is like being a style guru for your words. Those fancy loops and twirls are like adding stylish accessories to your writing. Just as the perfect necklace or bracelet can make an outfit go from good to great, your hand lettering can make words really stand out in an amazing way. Your fingers become little fashion designers, turning ordinary letters into a dazzling display!

3. Your Own Artistic Signature:

Hand lettering lets you be the artist of your words. The way you write creates a signature style that's uniquely you. Imagine your name becoming a piece of art—each letter is like a mini masterpiece, and together, they tell the world: "This is me, and I'm remarkable!"

4. Travel Back in Style:

Hand lettering is like having a time machine for words, but with a stylish twist! You can explore cool styles from the past and bring them into the present. Think of it as dressing up your words in vintage fashion. Learning hand lettering lets you be a time-traveling artist, blending the best of then and now.

5. Focus with Artistic Superpowers:

When you're in the zone with hand lettering, it's like having artistic superpowers! Your mind says, "Let's create something amazing," and your fingers follow suit. Hand lettering isn't just about making pretty letters. It gives you the opportunity to dive into a world where you're the artist, the director, and the star. It's your creative superpower, making you unstoppable!

So, awesome artists, get ready to sprinkle some magic, add a dash of style, and create your own artistic signature with the enchanting world of hand lettering!

About the Lettering Style

There are many different lettering styles out there to choose from and several that I think are excellent for teaching cursive. However, none of them were exactly what I was looking for when thinking about how to teach young artists like you to easily turn your cursive into hand lettering.

They were all missing an important element. Either they were not versatile enough, the letter forms didn't connect well, the slants were too varying, the shapes were not easy for beginners, the style didn't translate into lettering well, or the entrance strokes were inconsistent.

In this book I have chosen to teach lettering using a handwriting style that I developed specifically for those learning cursive *and* hand lettering. It is different from the lettering style I use with adults, but I believe this style makes it easy to transition from cursive to hand lettering without having to learn completely new letter forms. It also takes into consideration several things that are important for beautiful lettering: shape, size, spacing, and slant.

How to Use This Book

This book was created with girls aged nine to twelve in mind, but I am excited for everyone, regardless of age, to discover something delightful within these pages. Inside, you'll find activities tailored to two skill levels, just for you.

LEVEL 1

Level 1 is perfect if you're still mastering cursive. Don't worry if it feels a bit tricky. Level 1 is here to help you become a cursive superstar.

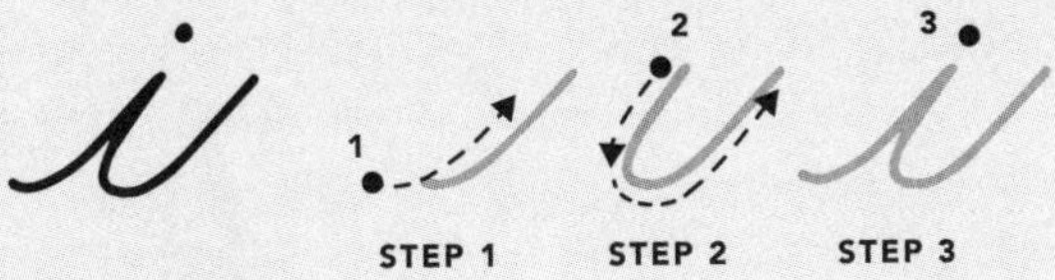

LEVEL 2

Now, if you're already a cursive queen and ready for a new challenge, Level 2 is where the magic happens. Dive into the world of hand lettering, turning your cursive skills into a canvas of artistic expression. Get set for a whole new level of creativity and fun!

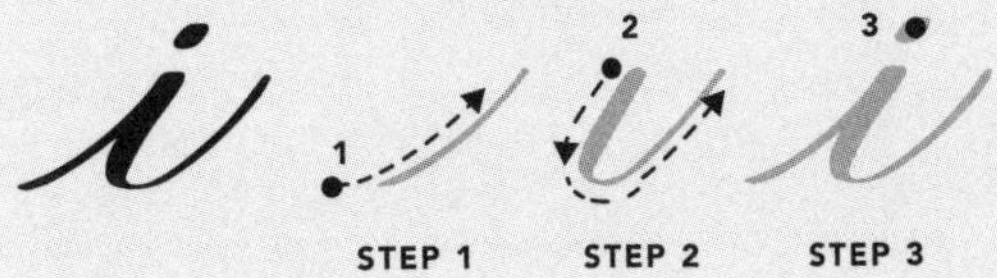

As you journey through these pages, you will discover cool coloring pages and practice sections. These are not just activities. They are moments to slow down, take a breather, and think about all the awesome things you are learning.

These sections are also meant to show you how to practice memorizing and meditating on God's Word through hand lettering. So as you create, let your creativity be a way to connect with God and think about how and why you were created.

Here's a little secret: It's totally cool not to finish the whole book in one go. Take your time, enjoy the process, and savor each new skill. Learning is an adventure, and I'm here to make it fun for you!

Setting Up Your Space

Let the magic begin!

Step 1: Gather Your Supplies

Make sure you have your trusty pencil or pen and some clean, blank paper. Set your supplies where you can easily reach them and maybe even turn on some of your favorite music! Some of my favorite pens for learning cursive are Pilot FriXion Ball Erasable & Refillable Gel Ink Pens, and my favorite lettering pens are Tombow Fudenosuke Brush Pens.

Step 2: Sit Comfortably

Find a comfy spot where you can sit up straight with your feet on the floor. Good posture makes for smooth sailing in the world of cursive.

Step 3: Paper Positioning

Place your paper flat on the table or desk in front of you. Think of it as your blank canvas waiting for cursive magic.

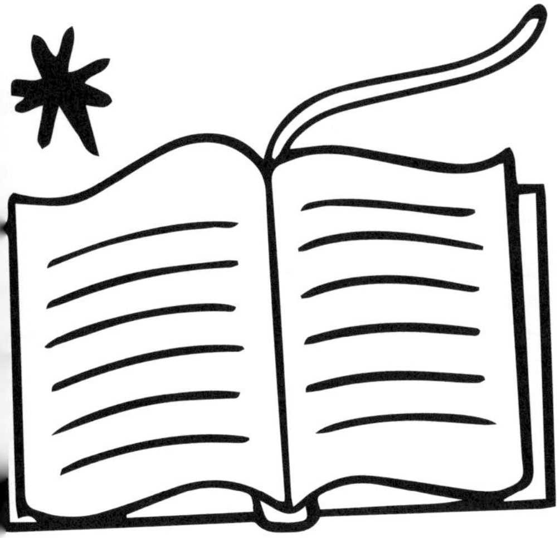

Step 4: Tilt the Paper Slightly

Cursive writing has a lovely tilt to the letters. Here's the trick: Tilt the top of your paper slightly to the left if you're right-handed or to the right if you're left-handed. This way, you'll have a clear view of what you're writing, and your hand won't get in the way.

Step 5: Get a Grip

Are you right- or left-handed? Whichever hand you favor, hold your pen in between the thumb and index finger, a little above the tip, with a gap in between. Left-handers should hold the pen slightly farther up from the tip. A relaxed grip is the key—not too tight, not too loose.

Step 6: Ready, Set, Cursive!

Now that your paper is in place and you are all set up, dive into the cursive sea. Let those letters flow and have a blast on your hand lettering adventure!

Remember, practice makes progress, so enjoy the journey of becoming a cursive maestro!

Line Warm-Ups

Cursive writing is connected by one smooth movement. Instead of picking up your pen and starting a new letter, each letter is connected to the one before it. Try tracing these patterns to get your hands ready for writing!

Basic Strokes

Hand lettering is a bit like writing in cursive, but with a fun twist: You get to make your strokes different sizes. *Strokes* is just a fancy word for the lines you draw!

When your pen goes up, make it like a fairy's touch—very light and thin. Now, when it goes down, give it a superhero landing—bold and thick. So remember, thin for up, thick for down. You're turning your letters into art superheroes!

Use your brush pen to form downstrokes in the space provided. Remember to apply pressure to the pen to achieve the thick stroke.

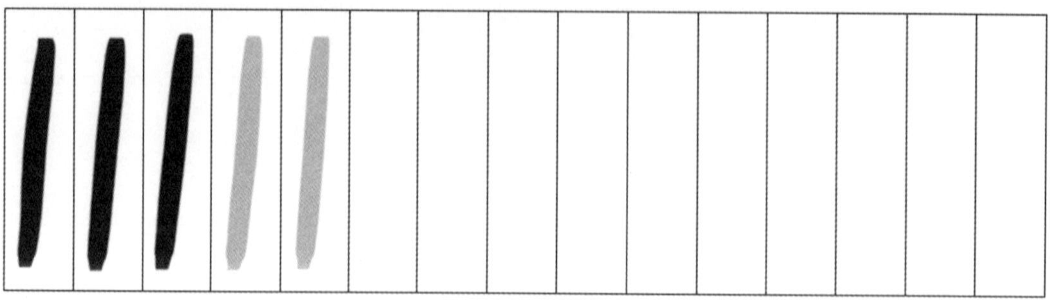

Now practice your upstrokes following the example below. You want to use light pressure to create a thin, delicate line.

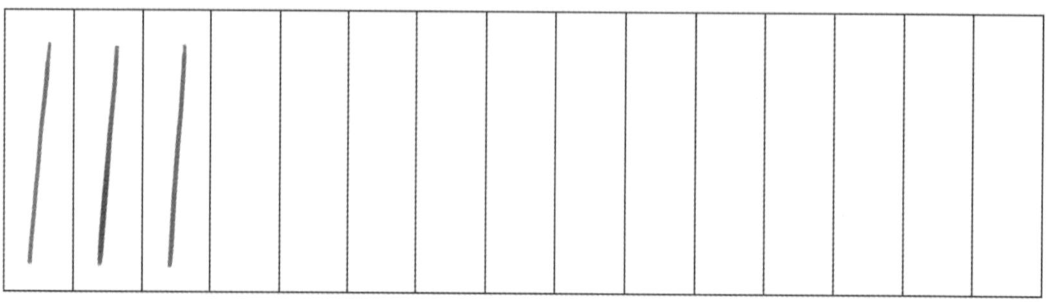

Putting your upstrokes and downstrokes together, you are going to create loops, waves, and curves to help solidify your understanding of how pressure affects your strokes.

The Basic Strokes

There are eight basic strokes we will be learning. Did you know that you can create almost every letter form with these eight basic strokes? Learn to master these and you will be a pro in no time!

Copy the patterns below on the lines provided.

The Entry Stroke

The Underturn

The Overturn

The Compound Curve

The Oval

The Reverse Oval

The Ascending Loop

The Descending Loop

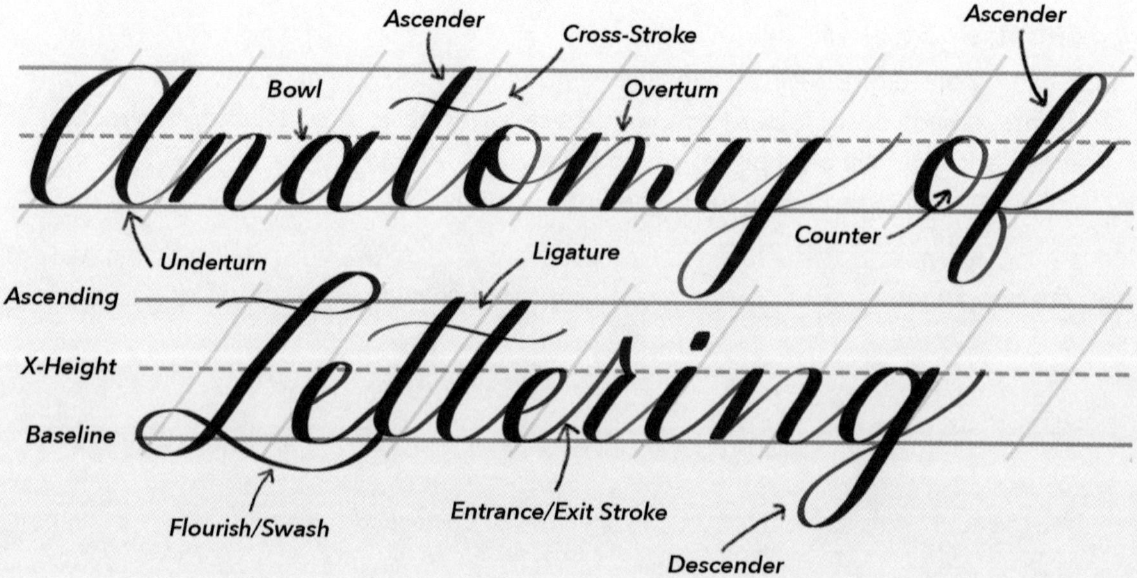

Letter Practice: Letter Groupings

You might notice that the order of letters in this book isn't alphabetical. I planned it this way so you can learn letters in groups that share similar formation patterns and gradually increase in difficulty.

Letter Practice: Height Chart

Look at this lowercase alphabet. Some letters are tall, and others are shorter. Notice where each letter sits on the lines.

The tops of tall letters reach the highest line, like *b*.

It's important to take notice on which line each letter starts and ends.

PART 1

LOWERCASE LETTERS

LESSON 1

Making Waves

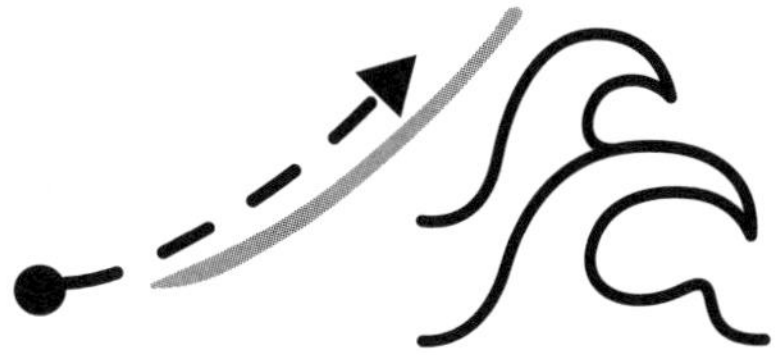

These letters all begin with normal entry strokes starting at the baseline and moving upward with a slight undercurve to the x-height.

i u w y n m v e r s j p t

LEVEL 1 Practice

Trace the letter in the direction of the arrow starting at step 1.

LEVEL 2 Practice

Using thick strokes going down and thin strokes going up, write the letter.

i

1

i i i

2

i i i

u

1 

2 

w

1 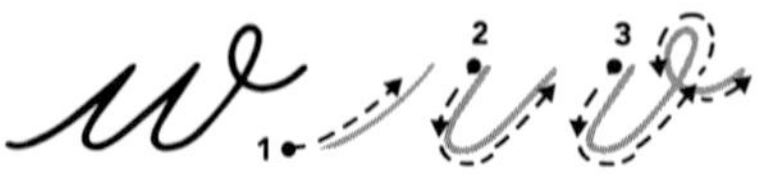

2 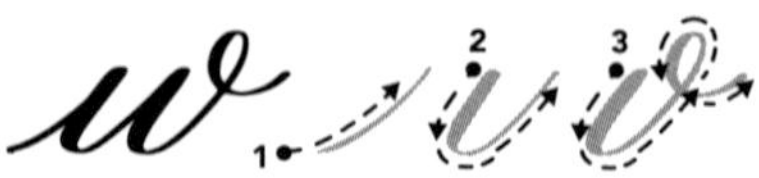

y

n

m

1 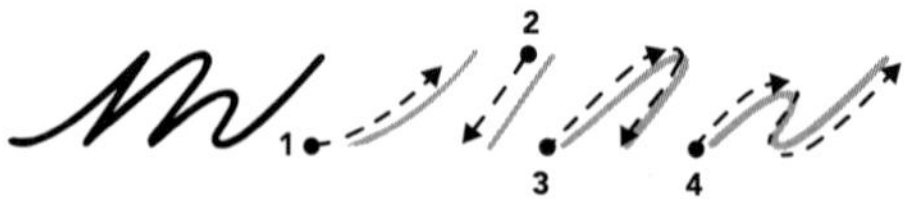

2 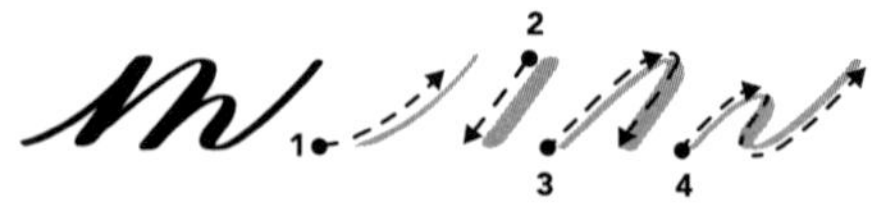

v

1 

2 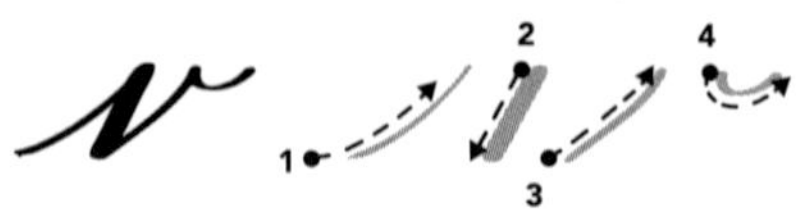

e

r

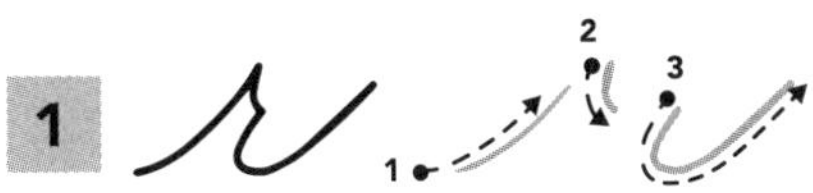

s

j

p

1 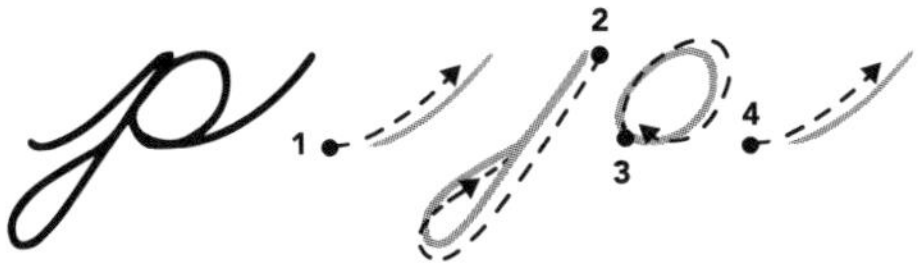

2 

t

1 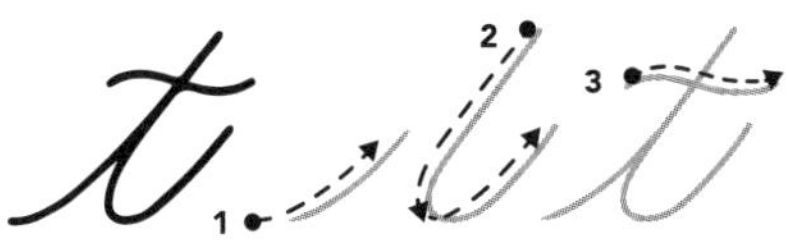

2 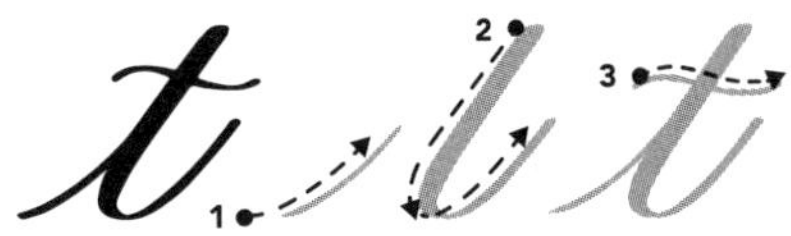

Writing Practice

Using the letters we have learned, complete the following words:

image

wise

new

promise

sweet

embrace

rescue

renew

DEVOTION

Searching for Belonging

We are all born with a desire to belong. We want to fit in, to be noticed, and to be admired for what we can do or what we look like. It feels good to have someone like you or compliment you. But it can be exhausting trying to keep up with what is popular or what you need to do to be accepted. The world tells us that we must look a certain way, act a certain way, or have certain things to belong.

It is good to discover a talent and use your potential. But your significance is not dependent on your abilities or your possessions. And of course, we know that having the right outfit is not true belonging. Or do we?

If only finding lasting acceptance were as easy as having the right clothes or being the first one to have a cell phone. But the truth is, those things do not secure the belonging we are all looking for!

If we live, it's to honor the Lord. And if we die, it's to honor the Lord. So whether we live or die, we belong to the Lord.

ROMANS 14:8 NLT

So, my brothers and sisters, you also died to the law through the body of Christ, that you might belong to another, to him who was raised from the dead, in order that we might bear fruit for God.

ROMANS 7:4 NIV

According to God's Word, we were made to belong to Jesus. In Christ, we can find true belonging by being fully known and fully loved by a God who gives us all of Himself. And because the children of God make up one body (Romans 12:5), when we belong to God, we automatically belong to our brothers and sisters in Christ. When we truly accept that we are loved by God, we can stop our futile pursuit of approval and find true belonging with God and His church.

Who are you if you lose everything that you feel makes you special? What things do you turn to for acceptance? Do you feel like you must earn God's favor or prove you are good enough for God?

Whether we live or die, we belong to the Lord.

Romans 14:8 NLT

LESSON 2

Tip-Top Climb

These letters all begin with normal entry strokes starting at the baseline and moving upward all the way to the ascending line.

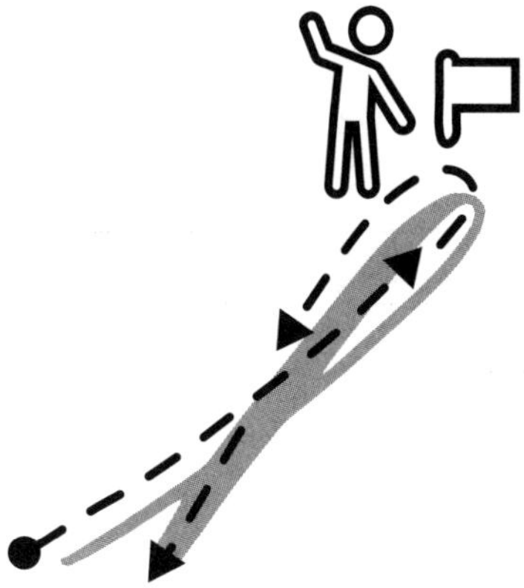

b f h k l

LEVEL 1 Practice

Trace the letter in the direction of the arrow starting at step 1.

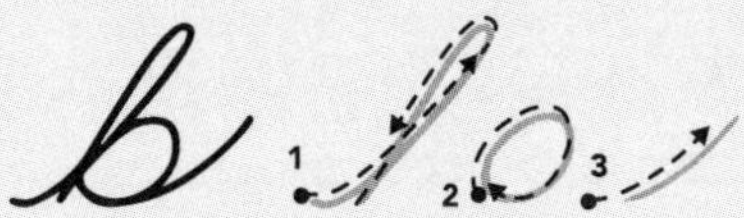

LEVEL 2 Practice

Using thick strokes going down and thin strokes going up, write the letter.

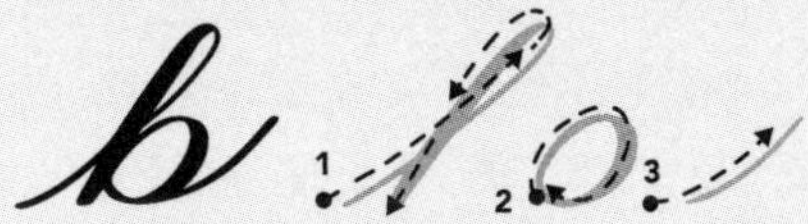

b

1

b b b

2

b b b

f

h

k

1 

2 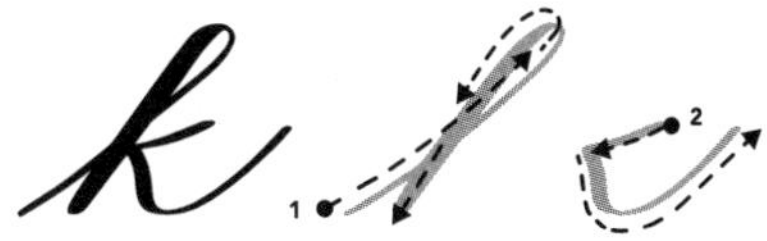

l

1 

2 

Writing Practice

Using the letters we have learned, complete the following words:

faith

flock

holy

bless

light

loved

DEVOTION

Never Alone

I remember as a young teenager fearing being alone. I did not like being separated from my family and, for many years, I had a difficult time spending the night away from home. I remember how thoroughly comforting it was when my mom or dad would come pick me up and tell me everything was going to be okay and that they were going to take me home.

I am sure that neither death nor life, nor angels nor rulers, nor things present nor things to come, nor powers, nor height nor depth, nor anything else in all creation, will be able to separate us from the love of God in Christ Jesus our Lord.

ROMANS 8:38-39

The LORD your God is living among you. He is a mighty savior. He will take delight in you with gladness. With his love, he will calm all your fears. He will rejoice over you with joyful songs.

ZEPHANIAH 3:17 NLT

In Romans, it tells us that nothing in this world can separate us from the love of God. Although we will have times of loneliness and heartache, God will comfort us and stay by our side. He will pick us up and quiet us with His love, assuring us that He is there and will never leave.

Knowing that we have unlimited access to God's love gives us the confidence to face challenges with resilience. We can get back up and try again. We can be separated from the familiar and feel complete peace and security because we know God is with us, and we trust that we have nothing to lose because in Christ we have gained all that we need.

How does it feel to know that nothing can separate you from God's love? Can you picture God singing over you? Rejoicing over you with gladness? Is that different than how you have pictured God before?

With his love, he will calm all your fears.
Zephaniah 3:17
NLT

LESSON 3

Backward Dives

These letters begin by starting at the x-height and going backward in an oval shape toward the baseline.

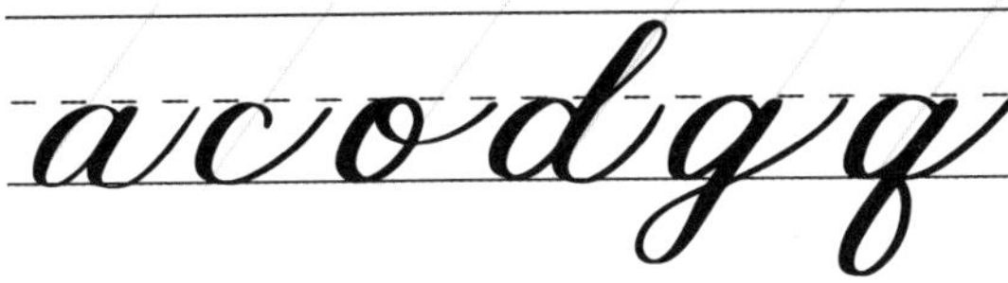

LEVEL 1 Practice

Trace the letter in the direction of the arrow starting at step 1.

LEVEL 2 Practice

Using thick strokes going down and thin strokes going up, write the letter.

1

2

C

1 

2 

O

1 

2 

d

g

q

1 

2 

Writing Practice

Using the letters we have learned, complete the following words:

dog

cat

cold

called

grace

quiet

DEVOTION

Renewing Your Mind

Did you know that there are things that influence your life and your thoughts without you being aware? Not only what you hear from your friends and family, but also through the music you listen to and the things you watch and read.

In our world today, there are thousands of things fighting for your attention and influencing your thoughts. There are even more if you have access to television, cell phones, or computers. Media companies need to capture your attention through advertisements in order to make money, and the best way they have found to do that is by making you addicted, isolated, distracted, and self-obsessed. What you watch or read affects your thoughts, feelings, and behavior.

Because we are so bombarded by things trying to capture our attention, it is extremely important for us to be diligent about renewing our minds. What does that mean? "Renewing your mind" means doing away with unhealthy thought patterns and replacing them with true, godly ones. You can start doing this by taking notice of thoughts and beliefs you have that don't line up with Scripture. You might even want to memorize or write down verses that help you fight the lies you hear most often.

Do not be conformed to this world, but be transformed by the renewal of your mind, that by testing you may discern what is the will of God, what is good and acceptable and perfect.

ROMANS 12:2

Reading and knowing God's Word is one of the best ways to renew your mind, but the friends you surround yourself with, what you listen to, and how you speak to yourself all play a part as well.

What do you say to yourself when you start to think you aren't pretty enough or smart enough? Do you fight that thought with truth from Scripture? Do the lyrics to the songs you listen to inspire good in your life? When you are with your friends, do they draw you toward Christ or away from Him?

Be transformed by the renewal of your mind.
Romans 12:2

LESSON 4

Over the Hill

These letters begin with an overturn stroke from the baseline all the way up to the x-height and curving back down to the baseline again.

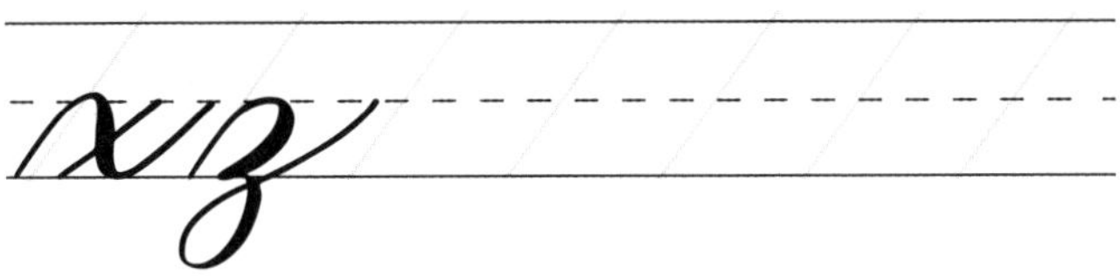

LEVEL 1 Practice

Trace the letter in the direction of the arrow starting at step 1.

LEVEL 2 Practice

Using thick strokes going down and thin strokes going up, write the letter.

X

1

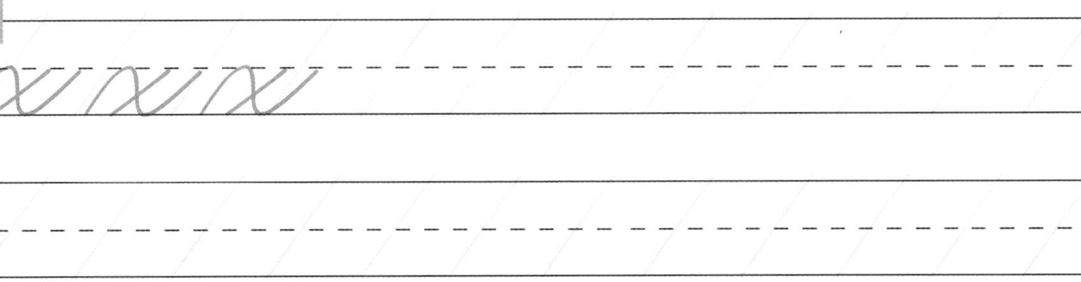

2

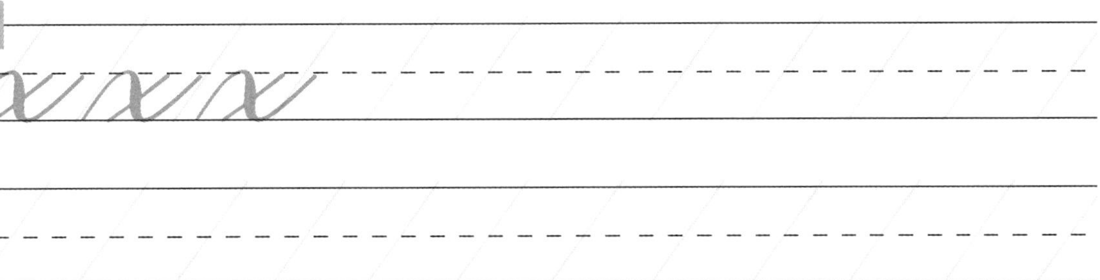

Z

1 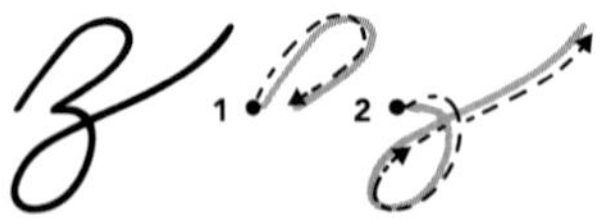

2 

Writing Practice

Using the letters we have learned, complete the following words:

zebra

box

DEVOTION

Standing Firm

Have you ever felt pressure to do something you knew was not right? Maybe you have been tempted to lie to your parents so you would not get in trouble. Or maybe you really wanted to say something mean to your sibling because you were jealous that they got to do something you did not. Or maybe you just felt like the world's way looked a lot more fun.

But you know what? Every time we give in and do the wrong thing, it always leaves us feeling empty and sad. Every single time. Why? Because God made us to find our joy in Him! And doing wrong hurts Him, harms us, and harms others.

Those who live only to satisfy their own sinful nature will harvest decay and death from that sinful nature. But those who live to please the Spirit will harvest everlasting life from the Spirit. So let's not get tired of doing what is good. At just the right time we will reap a harvest of blessing if we don't give up.

GALATIANS 6:8-9 NLT

Therefore, my bloved brothers, be steadfast, immovable, always abounding in the work of the Lord, knowing that in the Lord your labor is not in vain.

1 CORINTHIANS 15:58

When we give our best to Him, God remembers our faithfulness. Nothing you do for God is useless. So the next time you are tempted to do something wrong, stand firm! Follow Him wholeheartedly. When you feel something is wrong, run from the temptation. You are meant for something wonderful in God's kingdom!

Yes, my soul, find rest in God; my hope comes from him. Truly he is my rock and my salvation; he is my fortress, I will not be shaken.

PSALM 62:5-6 NIV

Have you ever done something you regretted?
What are some things you can do to strengthen your faith?

He is my fortress,
I will not be shaken.
Psalm 62:6
NIV

PART 2

UPPERCASE LETTERS

LESSON 5

Cliff-Hangers

These letters begin at the ascending line and move downward at an angle all the way to the baseline.

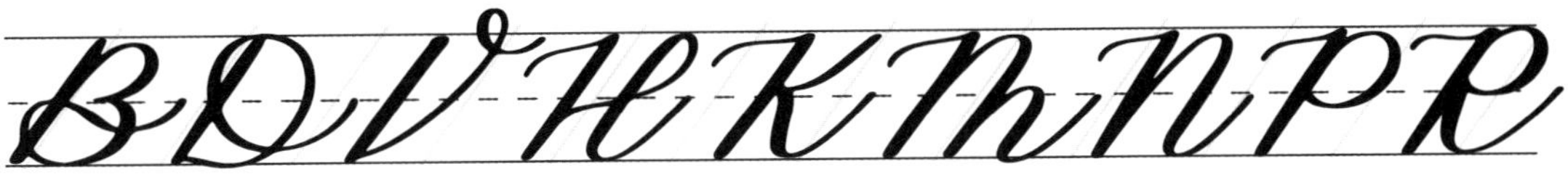

LEVEL 1 Practice

Trace the letter in the direction of the arrow starting at step 1.

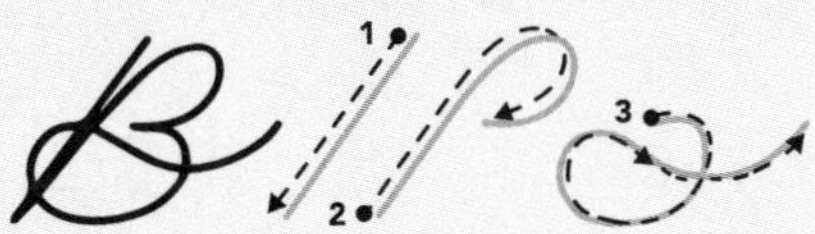

LEVEL 2 Practice

Using thick strokes going down and thin strokes going up, write the letter.

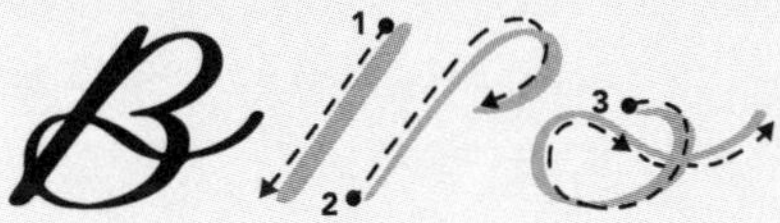

B

1

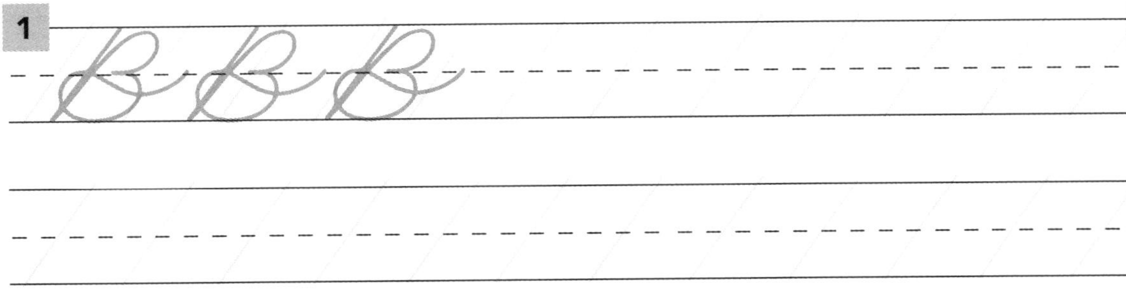

2

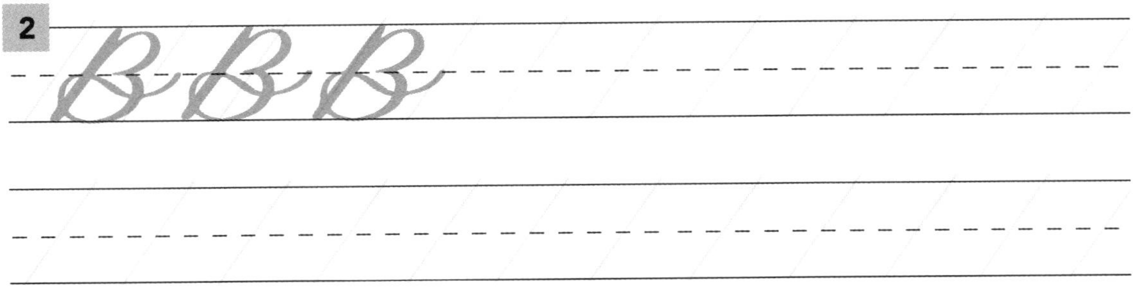

D

1 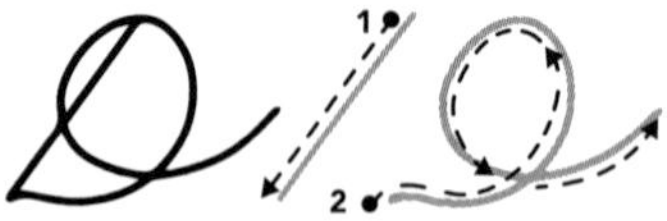

2 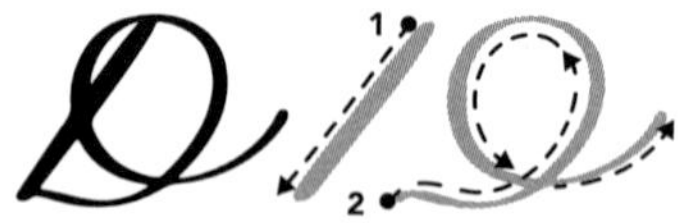

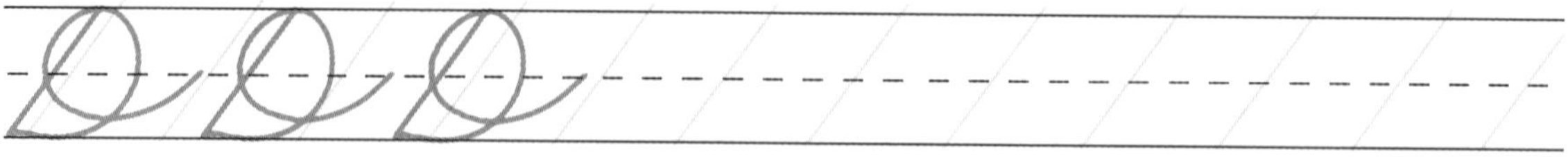

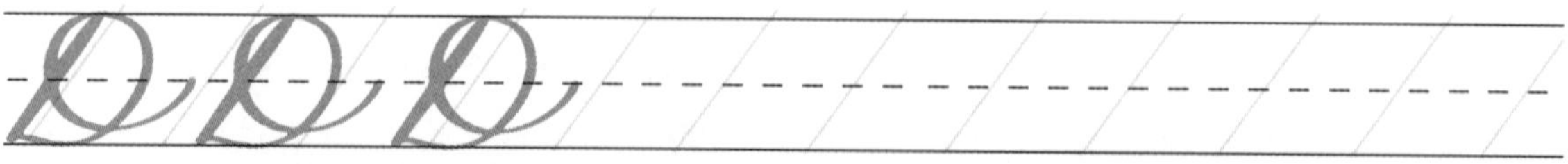

V

1 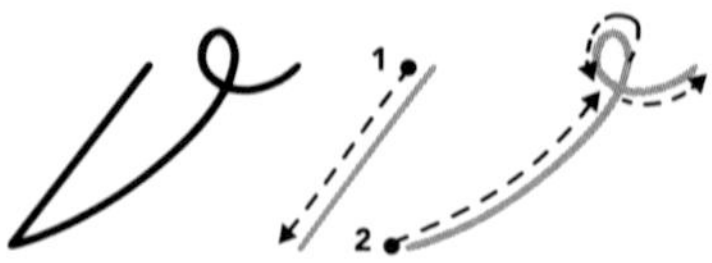

2 

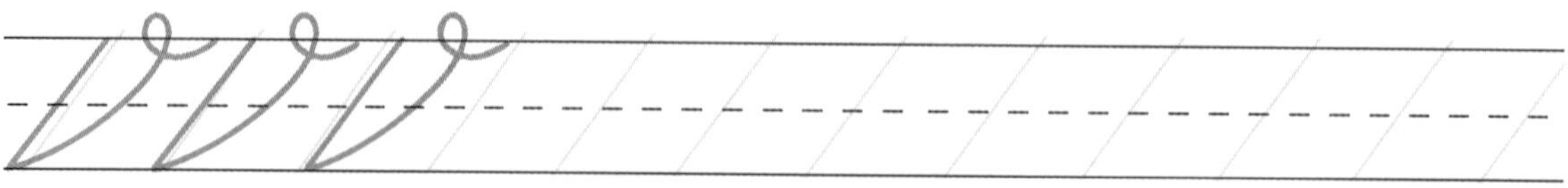

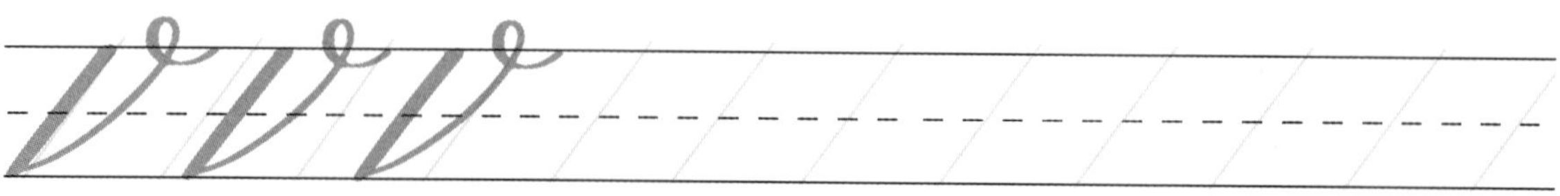

H

1 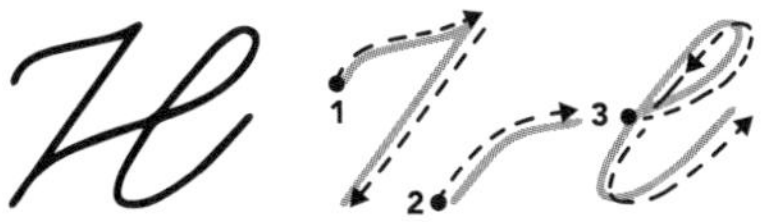

2 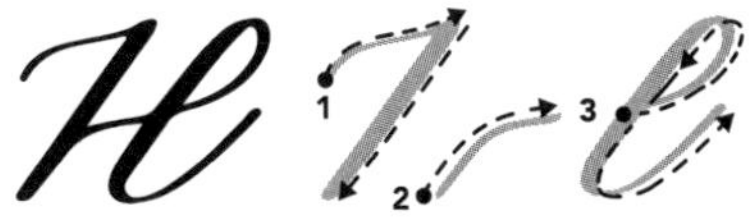

K

1 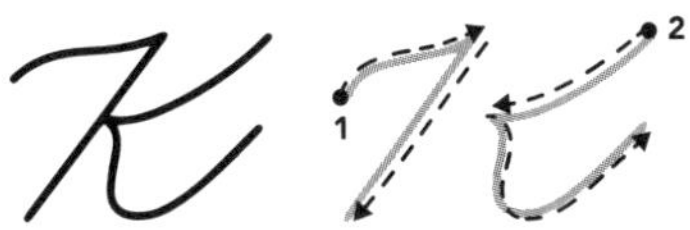

2 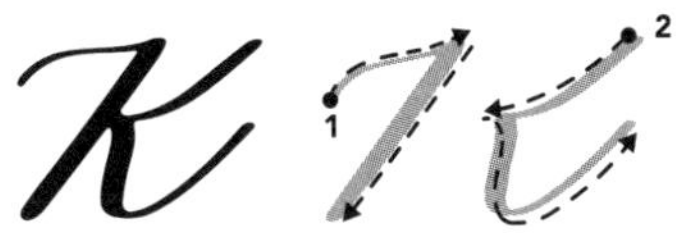

M

1 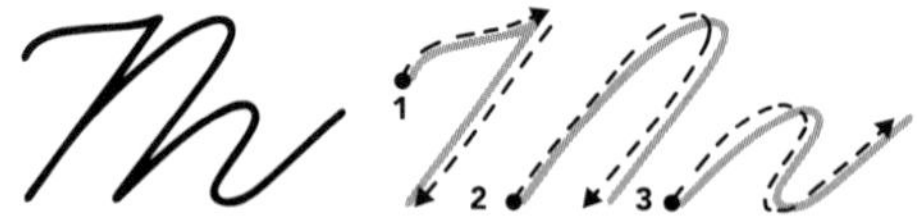 2 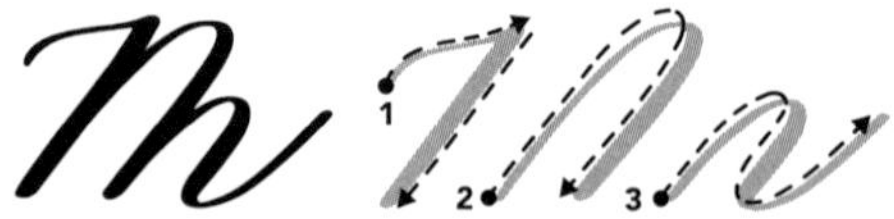

N

1  2 

P

1 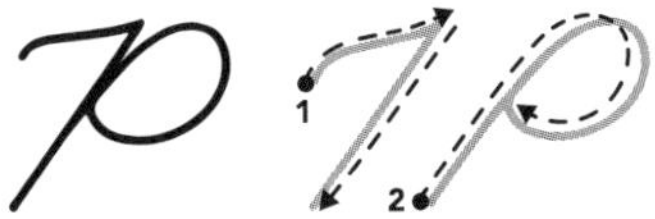

2 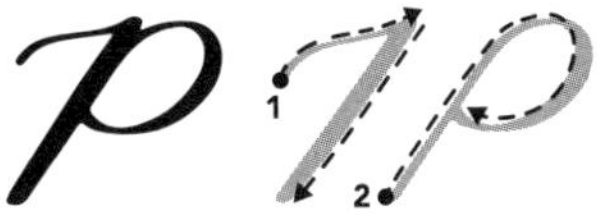

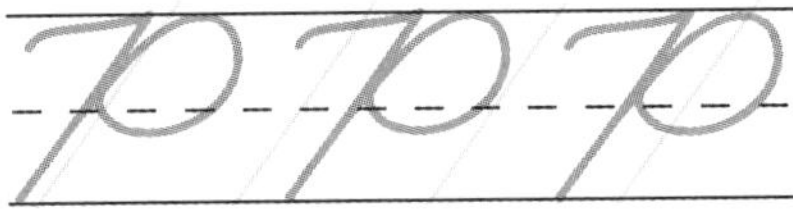

R

1 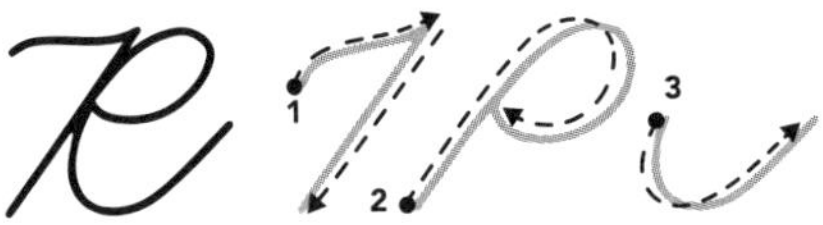

2 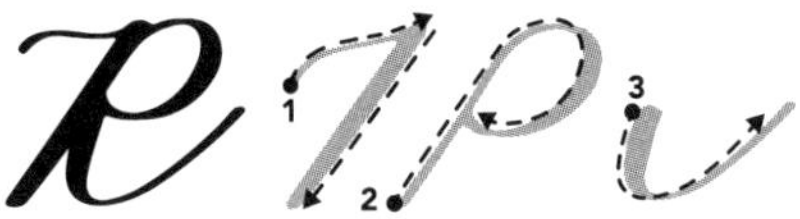

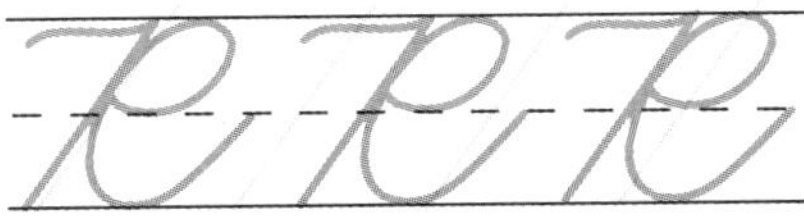

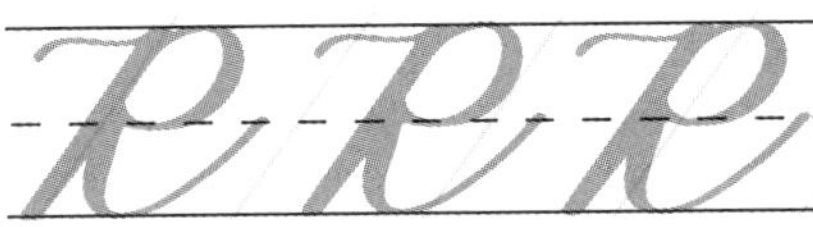

Writing Practice

Using the letters we have learned, complete the following words:

Why

Vow

Brave

Devotion

Rejoice

Peace

New

Kindness

Hug

DEVOTION

Forgiven and Redeemed

Imagine that you had a cameraman who followed you around all day, every day, filming you. Now, you might be thinking, "Oh awesome! I'm like a YouTuber or an influencer or a movie star!" No, no, no, I don't mean they film you for a little bit and then you edit out all the bad parts and then publish the best parts online. I mean that they film everything you do, all day, every day, including all your worst moments and your mistakes.

How would that make you feel? What if they took those videos every day and pointed out all your mistakes to you and to everyone around you? I would feel so ashamed, sad, and vulnerable.

There have been times in my life that I thought God was like the cameraman. I thought He was the one following me around, looking for ways to use my sin and hold it over me. But that is not what Scripture says of God.

> *But God is so rich in mercy, and he loved us so much, that even though we were dead because of our sins, he gave us life when he raised Christ from the dead. (It is only by God's grace that you have been saved!)*
>
> EPHESIANS 2:4-5 NLT

God does not delight in our sin. It does not make Him happy to see us mess up (Ezekiel 33:11). But there *is* someone I can think of who would be thrilled to see us mess up. The devil, or the evil one, the enemy of our soul, loves to shame us and loves for us to confuse his voice with the truth (1 Peter 5:8).

Because of what Jesus has done for us, when we ask for forgiveness, God forgets our sins and doesn't look back. He goes after the cameraman (the devil) and deletes the video. There is no longer any evidence of our mistakes or anything for the devil to hold over us (Isaiah 44:22).

God's grace is freely given, and His mercies are new every morning. This means you have the chance every day to ask for His forgiveness and receive His steadfast, unfailing love.

What are you going to do today, in this moment, to draw near to God and place your hope in Him? Do you need to ask for His forgiveness? What are some examples of how you could show mercy to those around you?

But God
is so rich
in mercy,
and
he loved
us so much.
Ephesians 2:4
NLT

LESSON 6

Backward Dives

These letters begin at the ascending line and move downward with a slight curve all the way to the baseline.

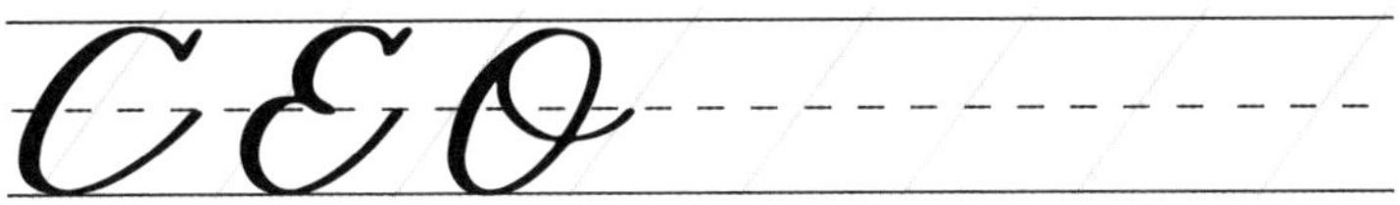

LEVEL 1 Practice

Trace the letter in the direction of the arrow starting at step 1.

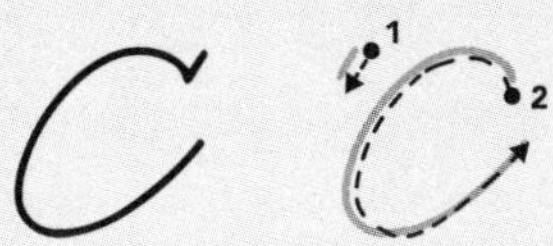

LEVEL 2 Practice

Using thick strokes going down and thin strokes going up, write the letter.

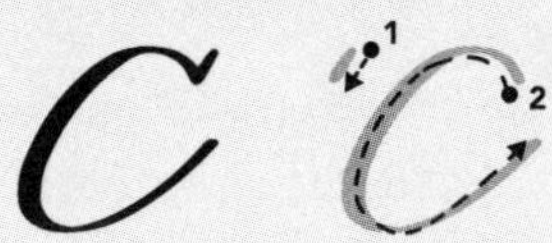

C

1

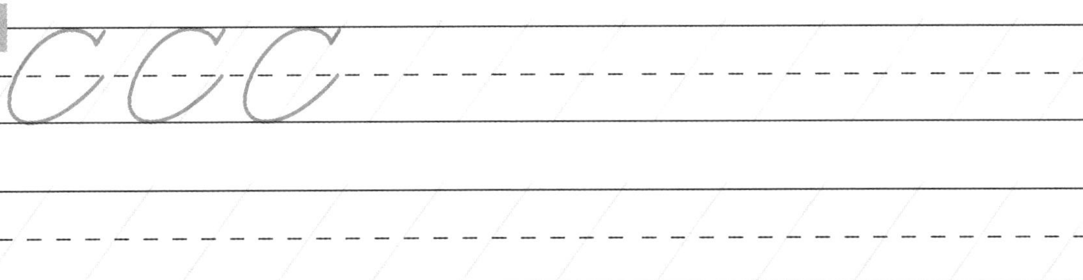

2

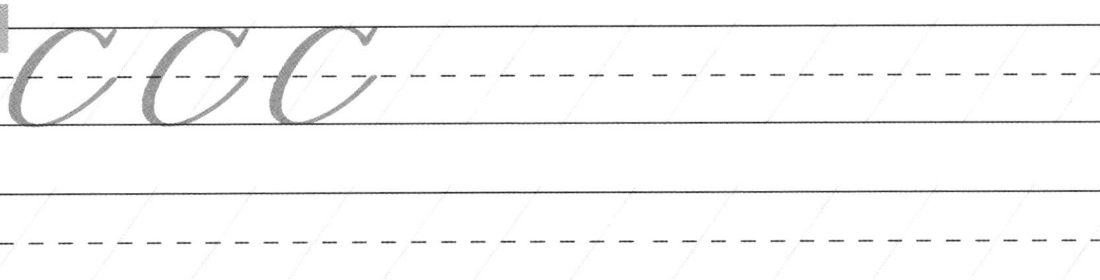

E

1 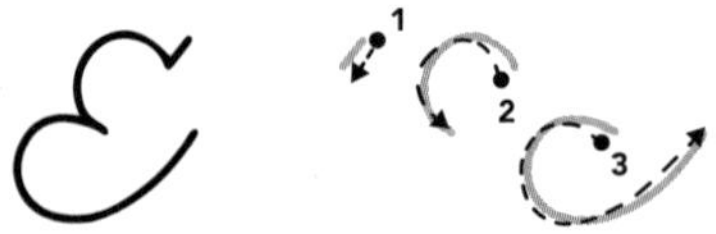

2 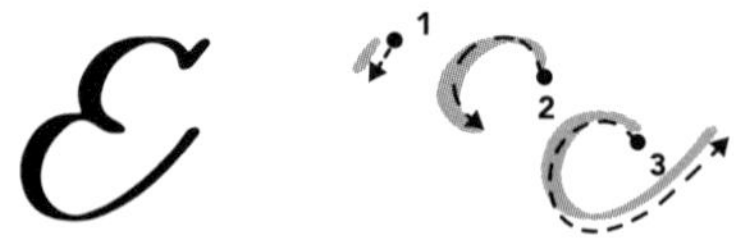

O

1 

2 

Writing Practice

Using the letters we have learned, complete the following words:

Oak

Cat

Encourage

Calm

DEVOTION

The Power of Friendship

When we go through difficult things, we often feel the need to do it alone. Maybe we feel like we should be able to figure it out, maybe we are embarrassed of what we are struggling with, or maybe we just feel isolated and like we have no one to turn to. But we were not made to do life alone. We were made by God to live in community with others who follow Him.

It can be difficult to be a good friend. When we are tired or stressed-out, sometimes the last thing we feel like doing is helping a friend or listening to them. However, we are called in Scripture to love at all times.

This is my commandment, that you love one another as I have loved you. Greater love has no one than this, that someone lay down his life for his friends. You are my friends if you do what I command you.

JOHN 15:12-14

A friend loves at all times, and a brother is born for adversity.

PROVERBS 17:17

It does not say a friend only loves when it is convenient or easy or when they feel like it. A true friend is there, even when it is hard. They will encourage and challenge you in your spiritual life. They will cheer you on in your successes and sit with you in your sadness. True friends are a prayerful people. Praying specifically for our friends shows a greater care for them. Prayer relieves the pressure we may put on ourselves to solve their problems or change their lives. Making requests to God on our friends' behalf cultivates a humility and dependence on the Lord for strength and wisdom.

If you feel like you are longing for a true friend, know that God hears every prayer you lift up to Him to bring godly community into your life. As you wait for His answer, remember that Jesus is a friend who will never leave you.

Do you have good friends you can turn to in a crisis? What are some other ways you can be a good friend? Let's invite God to encourage, equip, and embolden us to go out and become the kind of friends we desperately need.

A friend loves at all times.
Proverbs 17:17

LESSON 7

Reverse Loops

These letters begin at the baseline and loop up and backward toward the ascending line and back around in a curve to the baseline.

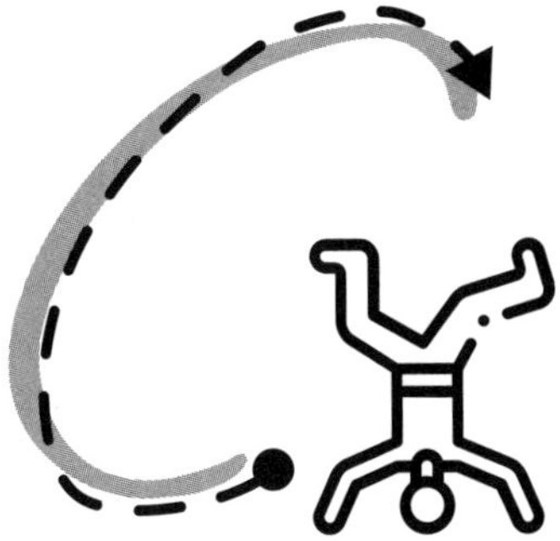

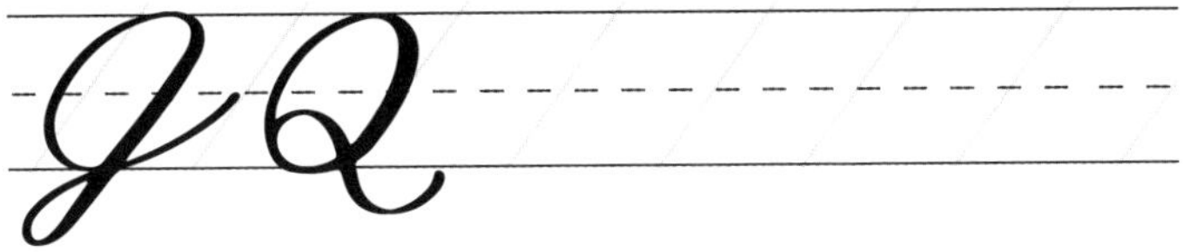

LEVEL 1 Practice

Trace the letter in the direction of the arrow starting at step 1.

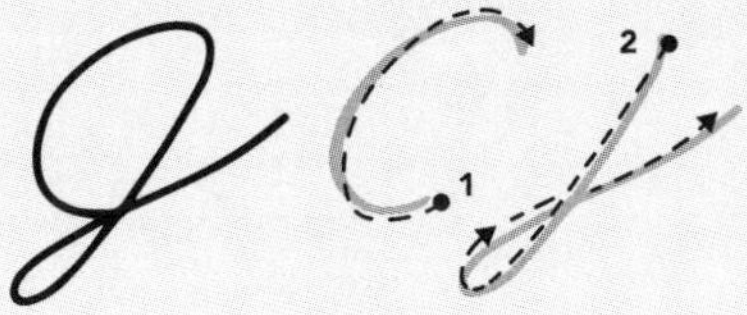

LEVEL 2 Practice

Using thick strokes going down and thin strokes going up, write the letter.

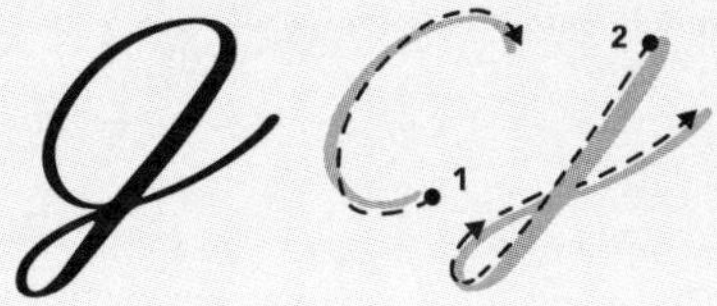

J

1

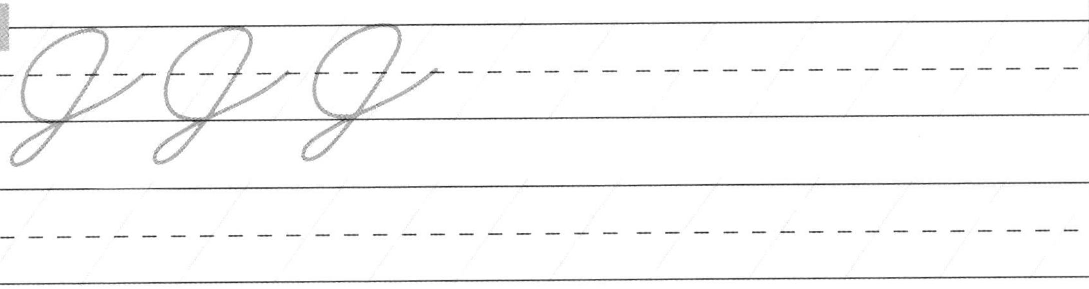

2

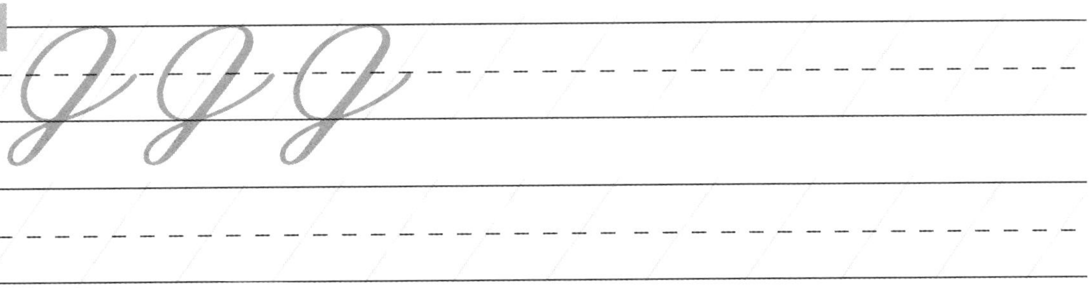

Q

1

2

Writing Practice

Using the letters we have learned, complete the following words:

Jewel

Joyful

Quiet

DEVOTION

Living in God's Grace

Have you ever received a gift from someone at Christmas and realized you forgot to get them something? Or has a friend done something nice for you and you feel like you need to do something nice to pay them back? We live in a transactional world. We give something, and then we get something.

Sometimes, in our relationships with others, our transactional tendencies bleed over and we seek people out to help us accomplish something or to get something from them instead of seeking them out to grow our relationship with them. But real love and real relationship happens when we focus less on what others can do for us and more on knowing them.

We can also become transactional in our relationship with God. It often goes unnoticed because the same action can be completely different depending on where your heart is at. You could be at church worshipping God, truly seeking relationship with Him. Or you could be at church worshipping God, hoping that He gives you what you want in return.

This transactional belief tries to earn God's love by our doing and being. If I am kind to others, if I am generous in sharing what I have, if I go to church on Sundays...then I will earn God's love and be worthy of His forgiveness. Our pride does not want us to admit that we have nothing to offer God in exchange for His love and forgiveness. We have nothing to trade Him to have access to His blessing.

And that's because everything we receive from God is a gift, given not because of our actions but simply because He loves us.

By grace you have been saved through faith. And this is not your own doing; it is the gift of God, not a result of works, so that no one may boast.

EPHESIANS 2:8-9

When we stop hoping only for God to give us what we want and instead search God out because we want to know Him, it turns our relationship with Him from transactional to transformational.

Are you approaching God as a Father or as a vending machine? Do you want a deeper relationship with Him or are you just seeking what God can do for you?

For by grace you have been saved.
Ephesians 2:8

LESSON 8

Wave Riders

These letters start by making a wave across the ascending line and then looping up and heading straight down to the baseline.

LEVEL 1 Practice

Trace the letter in the direction of the arrow starting at step 1.

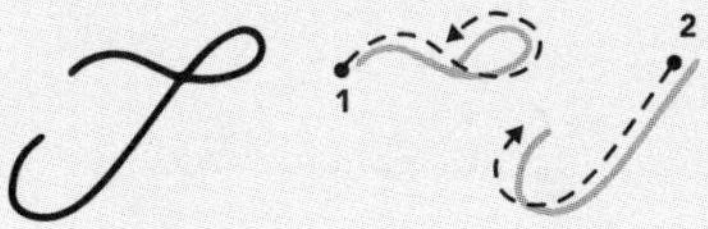

LEVEL 2 Practice

Using thick strokes going down and thin strokes going up, write the letter.

1

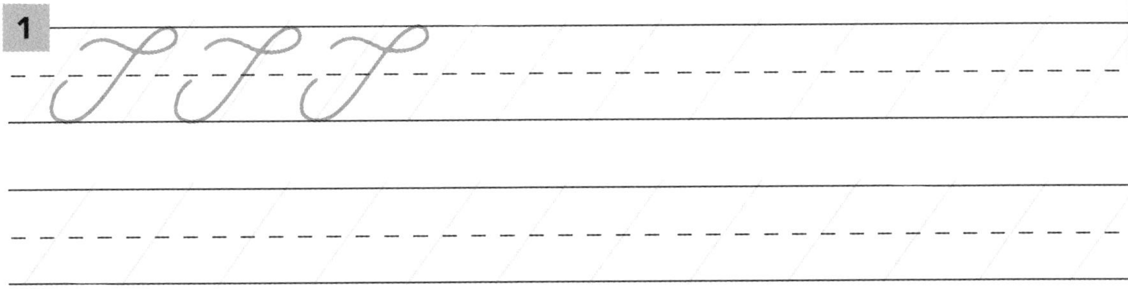

2

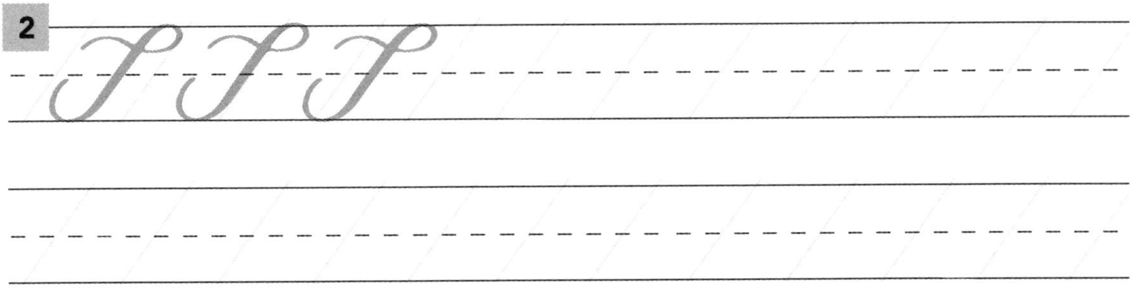

F

1 2

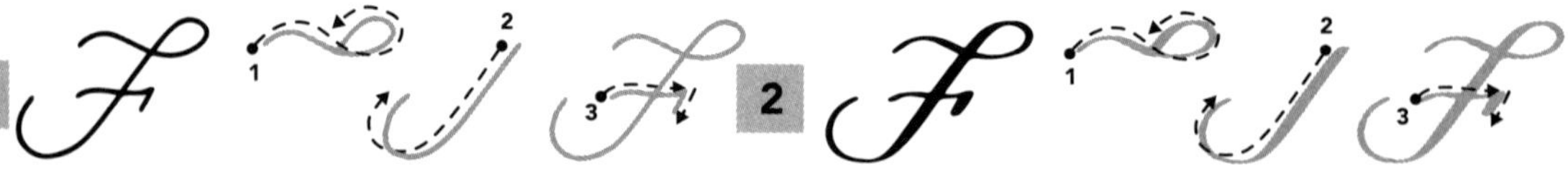

L

1 2

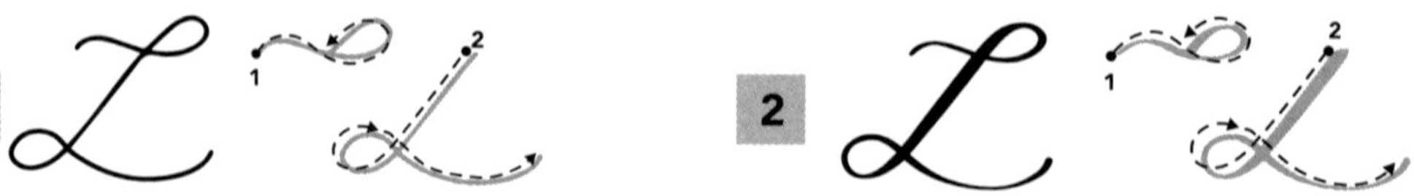

Writing Practice

Using the letters we have learned, complete the following words:

Love

Faith

Thankful

Learn

DEVOTION

Making Room in Our Hearts

I heard something recently that left me speechless. Someone said, "It is very hypocritical for someone to claim they want to spend eternity with Jesus when they will not spend five minutes with Him now."

Why is it so difficult for us to spend time with Jesus? Because we do not want to give up our time, our comforts, the things that seem so important to us. We like quick fixes and fast growth, so we tend to put off anything deeper to some future date: "When I finish this paper..." "When school gets out this summer..." "When life slows down a bit..." But that "when" never comes around because Jesus was never really our priority.

Commitment to anything takes sacrifice and endurance. Our hearts are not a hotel room for Jesus to come and go when we want. He is not satisfied living in the basement of your life, only coming upstairs when you need Him or when it's convenient for you. He wants to be a part of every room in your heart. He wants you diving into the depths of God instead of splashing in the shallows. Even more than that, He wants you to love Him more than anything else in your life, being willing to let go of anything that you love more than Him.

You cannot be my disciple, unless you love me more than you love your father and mother, your wife and children, and your brothers and sisters. You cannot follow me unless you love me more than you love your own life.

LUKE 14:26 CEV

That might seem extreme, but Jesus is trying to communicate the type of commitment and sacrifice He requires of those who follow Him. When Jesus calls us to a life of discipleship, He calls us to a life of surrender and self-denial in which we must give up anything that would take Jesus's place.

And you know what? The secret that Jesus tells us repeatedly is that you will be more secure and satisfied if you follow Jesus than you would be if you kept whatever you are holding on to (Philippians 4:19; Matthew 11:28; Psalm 107:9; Jeremiah 31:25).

What would be hardest for you to give up if God asked you to? Is it possible to grow and transform as a disciple without facing hard times?

And my God will supply all your needs.
Philippians 4:19
NASB

LESSON 9

Roller Coasters

These letters begin right above the x-height and overturn to the ascending line and then drop down to the baseline.

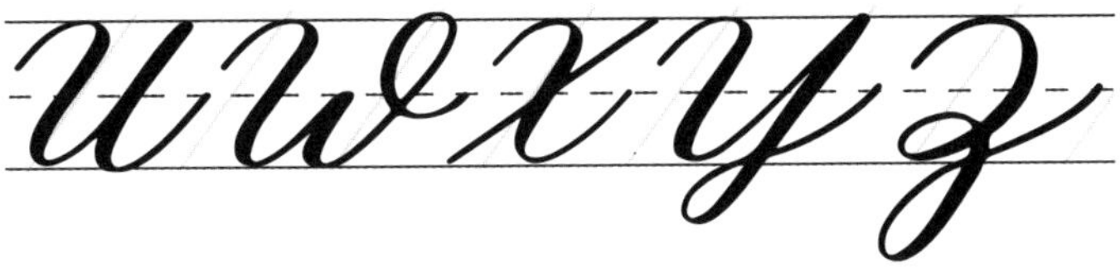

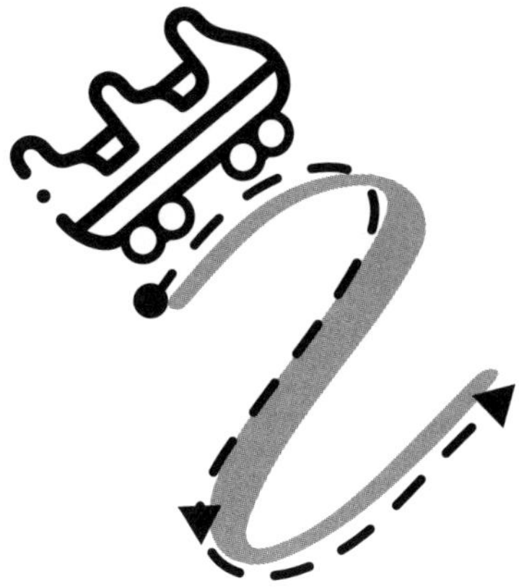

LEVEL 1 Practice

Trace the letter in the direction of the arrow starting at step 1.

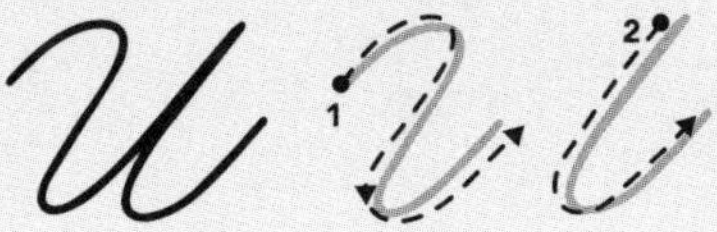

LEVEL 2 Practice

Using thick strokes going down and thin strokes going up, write the letter.

1

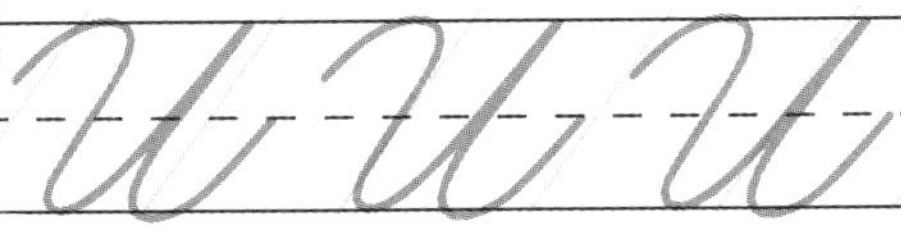

2

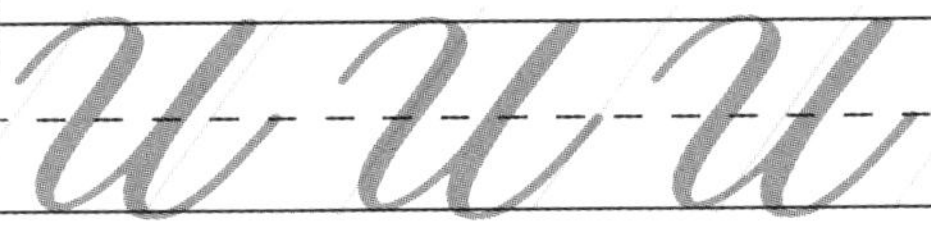

W

1 2

X

1 2

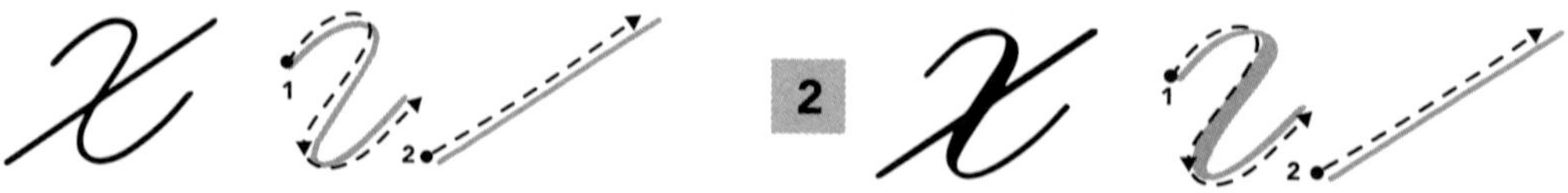

Y

1

2

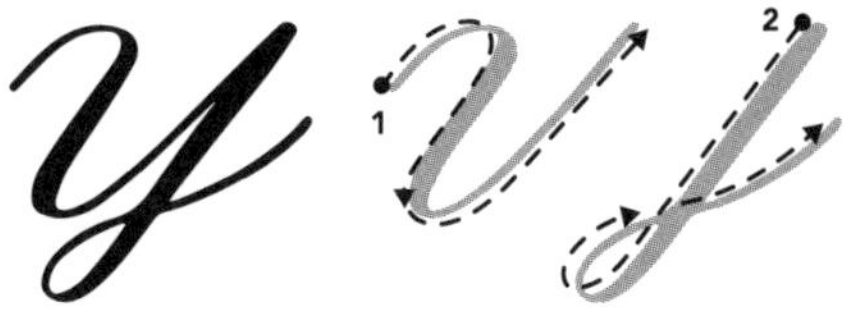

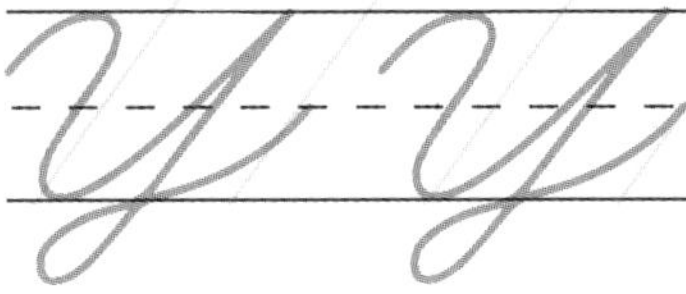

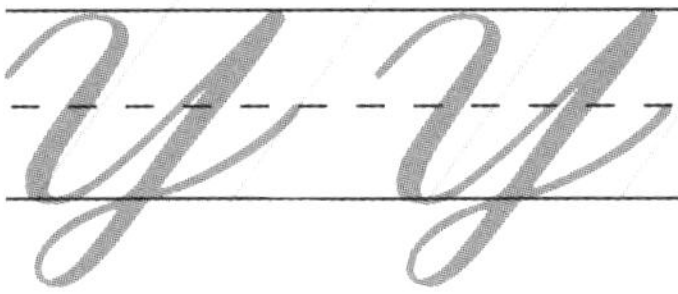

Z

1

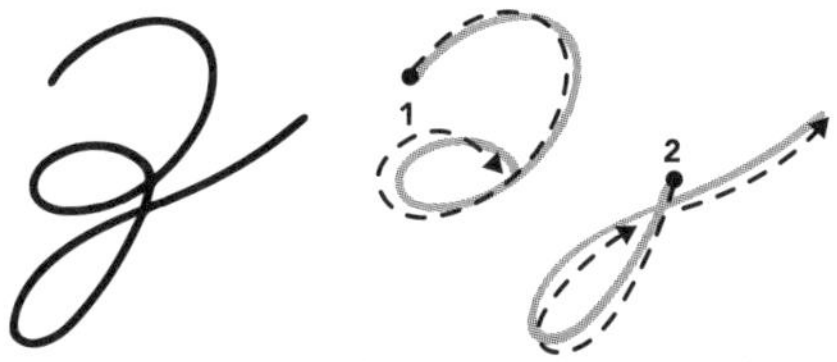

2

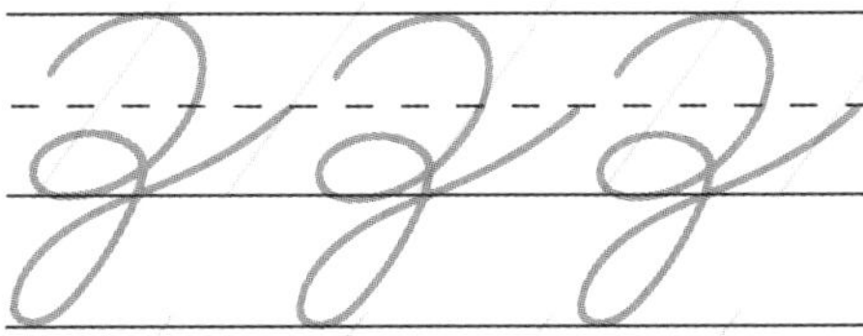

Writing Practice

Using the letters we have learned, complete the following words:

Utmost

Yearn

Wisdom

DEVOTION

Uniquely Designed

Did you know that no two fingerprints are the same? Not even identical twins have the same fingerprint. Each one of us is special to God and created in an awe-inspiring way. Everyone is important because we are all made in God's image.

You formed my inward parts; you knitted me together in my mother's womb. I praise you, for I am fearfully and wonderfully made. Wonderful are your works; my soul knows it very well.

PSALM 139:13-14

So many times, we don't like the image we see in the mirror. We are usually the first to point out what we do not like about ourselves or to compare ourselves to others. But God created all of you, not just the parts you like. You have inherent worth, regardless of your achievements. You are valuable because you were created in God's image. What do you think God sees when He looks at you?

God created you to be His image-bearer, but what does that mean? Well, it is kind of like being a mirror. We were created to reflect the image of God. Sin has broken and cracked our mirrors, so that image is distorted now. But when we repent of our sins and choose to follow Jesus, God's image begins to be restored in us. God's desire for our lives is that we would grow in holiness, desiring to restore that broken mirror so that we increasingly bear His image. This ongoing process of becoming more like Christ through the Holy Spirit is called *sanctification*.

And we all, who with unveiled faces contemplate the Lord's glory, are being transformed into his image with ever-increasing glory, which comes from the Lord, who is the Spirit.

2 CORINTHIANS 3:18 NIV

You are not random. You were created by God individually and purposefully. And His desire is that you would be holy, so that you would become a restored mirror that reflects His image (Leviticus 20:7; 1 Peter 1:16; 1 Thessalonians 4:7).

What are you thankful for in the way that God created you? One of the ways we can grow to be like Christ is by focusing on the fruits of the Spirit and asking ourselves, "Does this choice make me more loving, joyful, peaceful, patient, kind, generous, faithful, gentle, and disciplined?"

I am
fearfully
and
wonderfully
made.
Psalm
139:14

LESSON 10

Straight Climb

These letters start at the baseline and climb all the way up to the ascending line.

LEVEL 1 Practice

Trace the letter in the direction of the arrow starting at step 1.

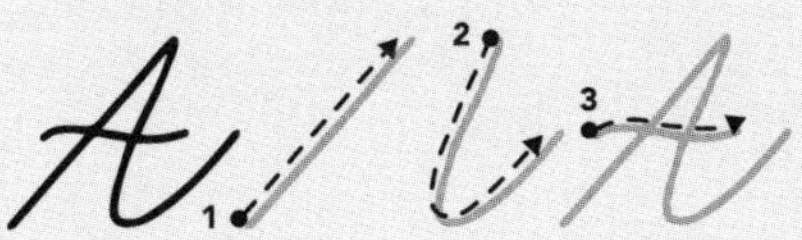

LEVEL 2 Practice

Using thick strokes going down and thin strokes going up, write the letter.

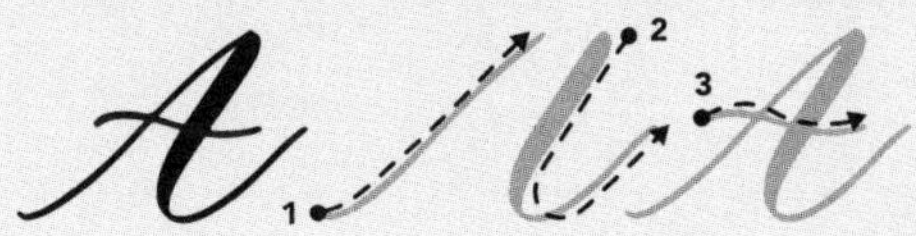

1

2

I

1 

2 

G

1 

2 

1 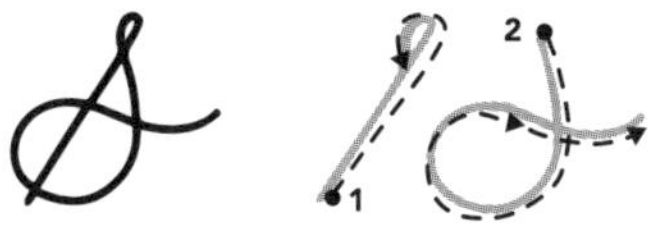

2 

S S S

S S S

Writing Practice

Using the letters we have learned, complete the following words:

Strength

Grace

DEVOTION

Confident in God's Plans

When I was younger, I struggled a lot with the thought that I knew more than my parents. I know, you've probably never thought that before. I did not always understand the decisions they made or trust that they had my best interests in mind. Or maybe it did make sense, but I still wanted to do it my way.

Have you ever disagreed with a decision your parents made for you? Maybe they told you to go to bed at a certain time or you were not allowed to have certain things and it felt unfair. I know I felt like my parents did not understand how important it was for me to go to Melissa's pool party in a two-piece bathing suit.

Maybe you don't always trust that those who look out for you have your best interests in mind, but we can confidently trust in God's plans for us.

I know the plans I have for you, declares the Lord, plans for welfare and not for evil, to give you a future and a hope.

JEREMIAH 29:11

Trust in the Lord with all your heart, and do not lean on your own understanding. In all your ways acknowledge him, and he will make straight your paths.

PROVERBS 3:5-6

Jeremiah 29:11 is well known, but it is often forgotten that this verse comes after God told His people, who were in captivity, to remain faithful and flourish while they waited for God to rescue them. He told them it would be 70 years before they could return to their homeland and then reminded them that He had good things planned for them even where they were now.

No matter how perfect our plans seem, it is usually what's not in our plans that ends up drawing us most deeply into the heart of God. Just like He did with His disciples, Jesus invites us to let go of our plans and follow Him. He wants us to "Come and see," inviting us to trust that His way is better. And, unlike I did with my parents, I will be the first to admit that His way is always better.

Do you believe God has good things for you?
How can you show God that you are surrendering to His plan?
Is there something that is distracting you from Him?

So give
you a future
and a hope.
Jeremiah
29:11

A NOTE FOR PARENTS

In an era dominated by digital communication and keyboard proficiency, the question of whether children should learn cursive writing may arise. While some may argue that the traditional skill is becoming obsolete, there is a compelling case to be made for the enduring value of cursive handwriting in a child's education.

Beyond its aesthetic appeal, cursive writing engages multiple cognitive functions and offers a range of unique benefits that contribute to a child's holistic development. As we delve into the art of cursive and hand lettering, it becomes evident that this time-honored skill is more than just elegant loops and swirls; it is a gateway to enhanced cognitive abilities, improved fine motor skills, and a deeper connection with the written word.

I hope this book has convinced you why encouraging children to learn cursive is not merely a nod to tradition but a strategic investment in their intellectual, personal, and spiritual growth.

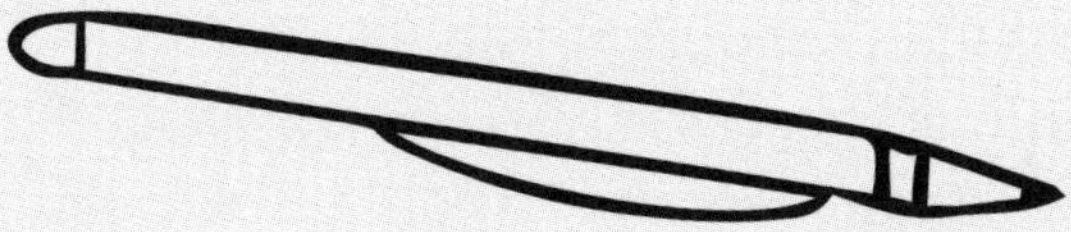

Why Hand Lettering? The Benefits of Cursive

1. Cognitive Benefits:

Cursive writing engages different parts of the brain compared to printing or typing. The continuous, flowing nature of cursive requires children to coordinate hand-eye movements and develop spatial awareness. Research suggests that this process can enhance overall brain connectivity, leading to improved reading and language skills.

2. Fine-Motor Skills Development:

Mastering cursive requires precise control over hand movements and muscle coordination. As children learn to form the intricate loops and curves, they enhance their fine-motor skills. This refinement of motor control not only aids in the mastery of handwriting but also lays a foundation for improved dexterity in other activities, such as playing musical instruments, participating in sports, and engaging in arts and crafts.

3. Personal Connection with Written Expression:

Cursive writing allows for a more personalized and expressive form of communication. As children develop their cursive skills, they become better equipped to convey emotions and ideas through the subtleties of their handwriting. This personal connection fosters a sense of pride and ownership in one's written work, contributing to the development of a confident and articulate individual.

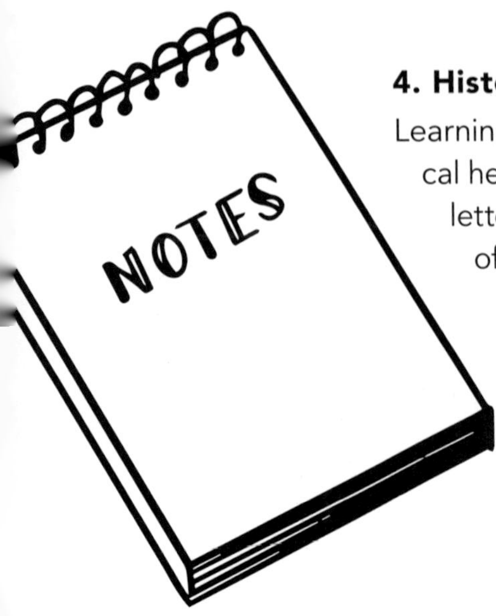

4. Historical and Cultural Appreciation:

Learning cursive provides a link to our cultural and historical heritage. Many historical documents, manuscripts, and letters are written in cursive, and exposure to this form of writing allows children to connect with the past. By learning cursive, children gain an appreciation for the evolution of written language and the cultural significance of various script styles. This awareness contributes to a well-rounded education that extends beyond the practical aspects of communication.

5. Enhanced Focus and Concentration:

The deliberate and thoughtful nature of cursive writing requires sustained attention and concentration. As children practice forming each letter and connecting them into words, they develop a heightened focus on the task at hand. This honing of concentration can have positive implications for academic performance and other areas of learning as children learn the value of patience, persistence, and precision in their endeavors.

Moreover, the careful and intentional style of cursive writing is perfect for diving into God's Word. As we take a moment to write Scripture slowly and thoughtfully, it allows our minds to truly absorb the meaningful words we are putting on paper.

The benefits of learning cursive extend far beyond the surface of elegant penmanship. This traditional skill serves as a powerful tool for cognitive development, fine-motor skills enhancement, personal expression, cultural appreciation, and improved focus. By recognizing the multifaceted advantages of cursive writing, we acknowledge its enduring relevance in shaping well-rounded, intellectually adept, and creatively expressive individuals.

Recommended Resources

https://www.zaner-bloser.com/HW21Summit/index.html and other resources at Zaner-Bloser.com
https://nha-handwriting.org.uk

References

Dinehart, Laura H. "Handwriting in early childhood education: Current research and future implications," *Journal of Early Childhood Literacy* 15, no. 1 (2014): 97-118, https://doi.org/10.1177/1468798414522825.

Mueller, Pam A. and Daniel M. Oppenheimer, "The Pen Is Mightier Than the Keyboard: Advantages of Longhand Over Laptop Note Taking," *Psychological Science* 25, no. 6 (2014): 1159–1168.

Saperstein Associates. *Handwriting in the 21st Century? Research Shows Why Handwriting Belongs in Today's Classroom*, 2012. https://media.zaner-bloser.com/hw21summit/public/H2948_HW_Summit_White_Paper_eVersion.pdf.

Vinci-Booher, Sophia and Karin H. James. "The Contribution of Handwriting to Letter Processing in Early Reading Development." In *Routledge International Handbook of Visual-motor skills, Handwriting, and Spelling*, edited by Yanyan Ye, Tomohiro Inoue, Urs Maurer, Catherine McBride, 97-110. Routledge, 2024.

ABOUT THE AUTHOR

Jenny Highsmith is an author, artist, and creative entrepreneur. Her books include *Every Day New* and *Hand Lettering God's Word*. She has a degree in visual communication and opened her own print shop in 2013. Jenny lives in Atlanta with her husband, Drew, and their three kids—Rowan, Conor, and Julianna.